SAMMY THE GOOD SPORT

Written by Tiffany Obeng

Illustrated by Eris Aruman

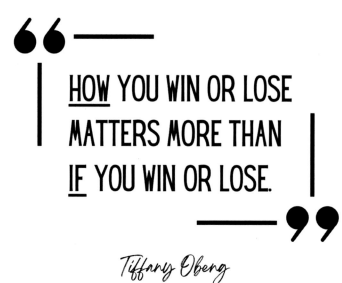

> HOW YOU WIN OR LOSE MATTERS MORE THAN IF YOU WIN OR LOSE.

Tiffany Obeng

Paperback ISBN: 978-1-959075-14-1
Hardcover ISBN: 978-1-959075-15-8
LCCN: 2023906296

And I like to win.

You know what else I like?
I like being a good sport, too.

And if I do not win,
I do not quit or make up excuses.

If I make a mistake,
I learn from it and try again.

And if someone else makes a mistake,
I encourage them.

And I try to be kind to others
because I like when others are kind to me.

BECAUSE I AM SAMMY AND I AM A GOOD SPORT!

Thanks for reading!

Want more great books?

www.SugarCookieBooks.com

Follow and Like on Facebook and Instagram

@SugarCookieBooks

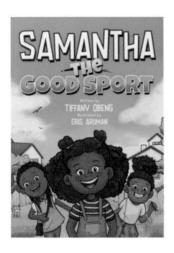 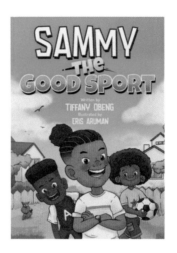

Career Books for Kids

- Andrew Learns about Actors
- Andrew Learns about Teachers
- Andrew Learns about Lawyers
- Andrew Learns about Engineers
- Andrew Learns about Scientists

Self Love Books for Kids

- My Summer Skin is Radiant
- Black Boy Hair Joy

Seasons Books for Kids

- Winnie Loves Winter
- Spencer Knows Spring
- Fallon Favors Fall
- Sonny Vibes Summer

SEL Books for Kids

- The Night The Lights Went Out
- Two Houses Down
- Scout's Honor
- Sammy The Good Sport
- Samantha the Good Sport

Spanish Books for Kids

- Andrew aprende sobre los actores
- I Have 10 Toes / Tengo Diez Dedos De Los Pies

Other Books for Kids

- I Have 10 Toes, Thank You Jesus
- Animals in the Forest Coloring & Activity Book

Made in the USA
Las Vegas, NV
22 February 2025

18514911R00021